CITIZEN SHE!

THE GLOBAL CAMPAIGN FOR WOMEN'S VOTING RIGHTS

HELVETIQ publishing has been supported by
the Swiss Federal Office of Culture with a structural grant
for the years 2021-2025.

CiITIZEN SHE!
The Global Campaign for Women's Voting Rights
ISBN: 978-3-907293-72-0
First English edition, 2022
Originally published in French as
Citoyennes ! Il était une fois le droit de vote des femmes

Text copyright Caroline Stevan
Illustrations copyright Elīna Brasliņa
Translated from the French by Michelle Bailat-Jones

Printed in China

helvetiq.com

CAROLINE STEVAN

CITIZEN SHE!

THE GLOBAL CAMPAIGN FOR WOMEN'S VOTING RIGHTS

ILLUSTRATIONS
ELĪNA BRASLIŅA

TRANSLATED BY
MICHELLE BAILAT-JONES

TABLE of CONTENTS

A LETTER to MY DAUGHTERS

DEAR DUNE AND SALOMÉ,

A few years ago, I let you miss school to join me in a protest march to support women's rights.

In the days leading up to the march, we talked—more than we ever had before—about the inequalities between men and women. You asked me why things were so unfair... and I had no answer. You were shocked to learn that in many places young girls are not allowed to attend school. You were astonished that even in the richest countries women are often paid less than men for the same job. But you've known for a long time that a girl might love playing soccer and a boy might enjoy doing the dishes. You've learned to love the word "feminism," a movement that asks for nothing other than equality.

We dressed ourselves in purple to suit the color of the march and we sang, chanted, and voiced our claims. That day I felt very close to the women walking with us, but also to those who had fought before us for rights that you and I now enjoyed.

I realized that I wanted to tell their stories but also tell the bigger story. Because on that march, Dune and Salomé, I realized I was passing you the torch of this fight for real equality. No longer just my daughters, you became my sisters in this great family of feminists marching forward.

GIRL POWER!

WHY DID WOMEN WANT TO VOTE?

Perhaps because they have a brain that can make political decisions and two hands that can drop votes into ballot boxes? Or would it be more complicated than that?

Once upon a time in a classroom...

The teacher enters, his shoes clacking across the floor. He's a substitute. He is very tall and thin, with a tuft of gray hair atop a head he turns every which way; he looks like an old heron, but less elegant. He's wearing beige corduroy trousers, a navy-blue sweater and pointy shoes that seem to perfectly mirror his beak-like nose. Leo studies the teacher's shoes because Leo loves shoes. He decides they're a little too narrow and not shiny enough. Jules is looking out the window. Emma draws on the cover of her notebook. Maria yawns, forgetting to put her hand over her mouth. And what about you? What are you doing?

Mr. Arbitrary—this is the teacher's name—clears his throat and starts speaking.

"Hello, kids, I'm Mr. Arbitrary and I'm your new teacher. I'd like you to introduce yourselves one by one so we can get to know each other. Let's begin here!" he says, turning his long neck to the left.

Maria opens her mouth, "My name—"

"Young man?" Mr. Arbitrary cuts her off, gesturing to her desk mate, Liam.

"But..." Maria stutters.

The teacher continues as if he hasn't heard her. "Now or never, young man."

Emma puts her pencil down and Leo looks up.

Mr. Arbitrary continues, "I would like all the boys in the class to introduce themselves, is that clear?"

"My name is Liam, I'm ten years old."

"What does your father do?"

"Uh, he's an engineer."

"Very good. Next!"

"I'm Sam, I'm eleven. My father is a chef."

"My name is Alexander, I'm ten. My father is a teacher."

Noticed something? Mr. Arbitrary isn't interested in any of their mothers' jobs. While the boys give their backgrounds, the children exchange surprised glances, especially the girls. Maria thinks that once the boys have finished, it will be the girls' turn. But no. When all the boys have finished giving their names, Mr. Arbitrary moves on to something else.

"Now we're going to change seats. Boys, you may choose where you'd like to sit."

The classroom falls silent. Wide eyed, the girls look at each other, trying to understand. The boys also seem shocked, but some are wearing bold smiles.

Emma raises her hand. Mr. Arbitrary ignores it.

Leo smiles at his desk mate, like a kind of apology, and leaves the table to go sit in the front row beside his friend Mohammad. All the boys have new seats within a few minutes: The three tables closest to the teacher are now full, and Jules has chosen a seat at the back of the room near the window and the radiator.

The girls begin whispering to each other. Mr. Arbitrary shouts, "Be quiet!" and speaks again to the boys.

"Now, boys, it's time to elect new delegates, boys obviously. Then, with my supervision, you must decide on the time and length of recess as well as the games you'll be allowed to play."

"But you can't do this!" Emma yells. This time, the teacher is obliged to look at her and reply. He turns his head from left to right, very quickly, his irritation visible, then takes a piece of paper from his leather briefcase. "Of course, I can. It's written here! These are the new school rules. Stop interrupting me."

He continues, "In the cafeteria, the girls will serve the boys and then eat whatever is left over. The boys will select the girls' uniforms, small size only. The boys will choose what sports will be played during Physical Education classes and in any case, the girls are not allowed to participate. They may, however, cheer the boys on from the side lines. The boys will come up with the schedule for parties and end-of-year shows. They will also decide whether or not to bring the girls along for any school outings. The girls must ask the boys for permission to spend their pocket money and of course to go to the restroom. The size of the girls' lockers will be determined…"

The tirade seems to never end.

"Any questions, children?" the teacher finally concludes, looking at the seven boys and ignoring the 14 girls. It's like they've become transparent, like they no longer exist. They are flabbergasted. No one dares say a word. Alexander, who has long believed in his superiority over the girls, finds the new rules completely natural. Jules thinks this is surely some kind of game but who cares; he's being given a bit of power and he'd like to enjoy it. It's obviously easier to be on the winning side.

Would you like to study in a class like this? I bet you think this kind of school couldn't ever exist.

Actually, this is pretty much how women have been treated for centuries. They were inhabitants of their countries without being able to voice any opinion on the rules governing the daily lives of all who lived there, including themselves and their children. Men voted for the laws, were the bosses, mayors, ministers, and presidents. Men had the rights and could decide that the women didn't have any. Men were able to go out, drive, study, and work. Women were not allowed to do this or had to ask permission from their fathers, brothers, or husbands. Even the size of furniture or cars was designed to suit the men.

It's easy to understand that women grew tired of this situation and found it unfair! Many had been working hard in factories or fields or raising their children. Some had spent years studying and were filled with ideas to improve their societies... In short, they were helping their countries move forward but unable to participate in discussions about how things should function.

And so some women decided to fight for the right to become citizens.

Citizens? A citizen is a person who has the right to participate in a country's political life by voting or by being elected. Suffrage, which is the right to vote, is how people select the representatives who then formulate laws. By choosing one person or another, you have an influence on the rules that organize your daily life. For example, there are laws that forbid cars from driving too fast or teachers from slapping students. In your city or town, it's the elected representatives who can decide to build a new playground or soccer stadium.

A ballot is a tiny piece of paper with incredible power!

HOW DID THEY FIGHT FOR IT?

The road to women's suffrage was diabolically long but there were a few women who paved the way right from the start. Already in 7th century China, Wu Zetian managed to become the empress despite this being a level of power reserved for men. Once established, she put policies in place to increase equality between men and women.

In the Middle Ages, Christine de Pizan, a French poet, claimed (in other words, demanded) the right to an education. At the time, and for a long time prior, it was felt that girls didn't need to go to school. Lucky for them, you say?

But starting in the 18th century, a group of women all over the world began fighting to obtain the right to vote. They didn't always succeed. Here are a few brave, bold, and inspiring examples.

OLYMPE DE GOUGES
1748–1793
FRANCE

Marie Gouze was born in the south of France, the daughter of a butcher and his middle-class wife. When she was 17, she was married off without her consent to a man 30 years older. She became a widow the following year and refused to remarry to focus on raising her son. Scandalous! She decided to take her life into her own hands, something which just wasn't done. Not at all.

Marie Gouze changed her name to Olympe de Gouges; Olympe was one of her mother's first names. The young woman began to write, following in the footsteps of the man rumored to be her biological father, who was an author and a marquis. She moved to Paris and published many plays for the theatre. Olympe de Gouges was very concerned with how little freedom women were allowed, but she also devised solutions to reduce the country's debt and help those most affected by poverty.

The French Revolution started in 1789. The people overturned the king and took power for themselves. Olympe gave speeches in support of her ideas. She was convinced that women would finally obtain the same rights as men but, sadly, even the revolutionaries sent them straight back to their kitchens! ⟶

Speak like men

Olympe decided on more action. In 1791, she published her "Declaration of the Rights of Woman and Female Citizens," modeled after the "Declaration of the Rights of Men and Citizens" published a few years earlier.

Article 1: "Woman is born free and remains equal to man in rights." Olympe de Gouges demanded the right to vote and eligibility for women, meaning the right to be elected; she also demanded freedom of expression. "A woman has a right to climb the scaffold*, she must have the right to go to court," she wrote, something which meant that if a woman could be condemned to death, just like a man, then a woman should be listened to, just like a man. Olympe never stopped criticizing the new government and its wrongdoings. On November 3, 1793, she was beheaded by guillotine.

Wake up, women!

Men, can you be fair?

*The scaffold was the wooden platform used in executions.

EMMELINE PANKHURST
1858–1928
GREAT BRITAIN

When Emmeline was 14 years old, her mother took her along to a meeting about the women's right to vote. It changed her life. In 1903, frustrated by the lack of progress within the pro-suffrage associations where she was a member, she and her daughters founded the Women's Social and Political Union. Their motto: "Deeds, not words." The group published a newspaper, collected signatures for petitions, and organized protests as well as "Women's Parliaments" for the days when the government, composed entirely of men, was in session.

Emmeline Pankhurst was arrested for the first time in 1908 when she tried to enter parliament to give a letter of protest to the prime minister. "We are here, not because we are law-breakers; we are here in our efforts to become law-makers," she pleaded. Emmeline would go on to be arrested seven more times, along with many activists who were with her, including her daughters. They went on a hunger strike to protest their arrest and were force fed using tubes through their nose or mouth, an extremely violent tactic.

On Friday, November 18, 1910, Emmeline Pankhurst asked the women now called suffragettes to gather in front of parliament. They were beaten up by the police and the day became known as "Black Friday," nothing like the holiday shopping event we know today. ⟶

MAKE EXPLOSIVES!

Emmeline decided that non-violent protest did not work and called for civil disobedience, which means breaking the law when a law is unjust, or for a good cause. The suffragettes smashed windows, set buildings on fire, and laid explosives around the country, making sure never to hurt anyone. From this point on, Emmeline Pankhurst wore a disguise or had bodyguards: A group of women, trained in jujitsu, called the "suffrajitsu". This was all the more shocking because women were considered to embody gentleness, never get angry or be violent.

The First World War was a turning point. Many jobs were taken over by women because so many men were fighting. In 1918, perhaps as a sign of recognition, British women aged over 30 obtained the right to vote. It took until July 2, 1918, for women who were 21 to be granted the right to vote, just like men. Emmeline had died two weeks earlier.

Educate girls

HUDA SHARAWI
1879–1947
EGYPT

Daughter of a politician and a slave, Huda Sharawi grew up in a harem, which is the part of a house reserved for the wives of a man, typically a powerful one. She was instructed to memorize the Koran—the sacred text of the religion of Islam—but was forbidden from learning Arabic, the language in which the book is written.

At the age of 13, she was forced into marriage with a much older cousin. She divorced shortly after because her husband continued to spend time with his first wife, but she remarried him when she was 21. During the years in between, she discovered opera, as well as literary and political salons, and met a number of European feminists. She became convinced that if women were allowed to study, they would be as powerful as men.

Huda Sharawi first founded a hospital and a school to teach health and hygiene practices to young girls. After that, she offered classes to teach them the alphabet—in other words to teach them to read and write. Later, she encouraged them to go to university.

Upon her return from a trip to Europe, she was getting off a train in Cairo when she lifted the veil that hid her face. A photograph of this symbolic gesture made its way around the world. At that time, Egyptian women were forbidden from showing their faces in public; just like Zorro or Batman, yes, except they had a choice.

Until her death of cholera in 1947, Huda Sharawi supported the campaign for women's rights. Because of her work, King Fuad I raised the minimum age of marriage for girls to 16 years in 1923, and the first female Egyptian students entered university in 1933. They obtained the right to vote in 1956.

BERTHA LUTZ
1894 – 1976
BRAZIL

Bertha Lutz was a Brazilian herpetologist. Herpetologist? This is what an expert in amphibians and reptiles is called. Bertha's particular area of expertise was frogs and lizards. Today, several species are named after her, like the *Dendropsophus berthalutzae*, a tiny yellow-green frog from the south of Brazil. As a child, she would accompany her doctor and naturalist father on his scientific excursions, and in this way discovered her vocation as a biologist.

Her other passion was women's rights, and her main cause was equality in the workplace: A man and a woman should earn the same salary for the same job. And also, obviously, women's suffrage, which Brazilian women earned in 1932. Before then, wives had to have their husband's consent in order to vote; single women and widows had more freedom.

In 1936, Bertha became one of the first women parliamentarians in the world. A parliamentarian is a person who votes and creates laws. Her first action was to create a committee in charge of checking whether the country's laws respected the equality between men and women. Unfortunately, Brazil became a dictatorship in 1937 and her project fell apart.

As the Second World War was ending, Bertha Lutz was one of four women among the 150 delegates who contributed to writing the Charter of the United Nations. She fought for the word "women" to be included in the phrase "equal rights of men and women" in the charter's preamble, and she won! I think Olympe de Gouges would have liked her...

LOUISE WEISS
1893–1983
FRANCE

Louise Weiss did nothing that was expected of her. Her father, an engineer, didn't want her to study, but against his will she received a literature degree in France and another from the University of Oxford in England. She was then told to become a teacher, a suitable profession for women at the time. Not interested! She wanted to work as a journalist!

With her organization "La femme nouvelle" (The New Woman), she encouraged an original and modern feminism. The word had not yet become widespread, but she became a queen of "happenings." The idea was to make a splash with a spectacular event so that the public would hear about the cause in question. In 1935, for example, she presented herself as a candidate in the municipal elections of Montmartre, near Paris, even if she didn't have the right to do so. She made her own ballot boxes out of hat boxes and collected nearly 18,000 votes! Together with her organization, the women released balloons and pamphlets over the stadium during the final match of the Coupe de France soccer tournament. They sent socks to senators with the words, "Even if you give us the right to vote, your socks will be mended." Indeed, many men believed that women would neglect their housekeeping tasks for politics. Another day, they chained themselves together to block traffic in the streets of Paris. Always with the slogan: "French women must vote." ⟶

ORGANIZE HAPPENINGS

In 1936, three women joined the government headed by Prime Minister Léon Blum. It was said that Louise Weiss refused a ministerial position. "I fought to be elected, not to be appointed," she is purported to have said. Do you see the difference?

During the Second World War, French women played a large role at work and also in the Resistance movement. The State could no longer leave them out, especially as most of the neighboring countries had already stepped up in favor of women's suffrage. In 1944, French women earned the right to vote and to stand for elected office.

PROTESTORS'

PAMPHLETS

POSTERS

HAPPENINGS

WOMEN MUST VOTE

MARCHES

ASSOCIATIONS

EDUCATION

SOCIAL MEDIA

PETITIONS

TOOLKIT

NEWSPAPERS

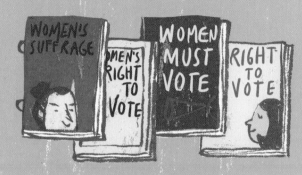

MANIFESTOS

EXPLOSIVES

THROWING STONES

CIVIL DISOBEDIENCE

COURTS

CONFERENCES

SPEECHES

LOUJAIN AL-HATHLOUL
BORN IN 1989
SAUDI ARABIA

Just like the English suffragettes, Loujain al-Hathloul knows all about prison. In 2013, she spent over two months behind bars after publishing a video of herself driving. What's the big deal, you wonder? In Saudi Arabia at the time, women were not allowed to drive. They finally earned the right to take the wheel in 2018, notably thanks to Loujain. Even before this, the activist was known for posting photos of herself without a veil on social media—something still forbidden in a country which gives very little freedom to women and polices their clothing.

In 2015, Saudi women were granted the right to vote and to run for office in city elections. Loujain signed up as a candidate, but her name was erased from the ballot. The following year, she was arrested again for signing a petition asking King Salman to get rid of male guardianship over women. Guardianship means that women are considered minors and must wait for their husbands to give them permission to do things, like you with your parents. A woman, for example, is not allowed to travel without her father or husband's consent. Loujain al-Hathloul was released but re-imprisoned in 2018. She was offered a chance at freedom if she would swear that she hadn't been tortured while in prison. She refused. She was finally freed in February 2021 but forbidden from traveling for five years.

TAKE THE WHEEL

ANTOINETTE QUINCHE
1896–1979
SWITZERLAND

Law was her thing. As you've just read, many feminists decide to break the rules that overly restrict their freedoms. Antoinette Quinche preferred to try to change them.

To do this, she began by getting her degree—the only girl in a class of boys. She was one of the first women to become a lawyer in the Swiss canton of Vaud. She gave free legal advice to women who needed it, fought to improve the conditions for women prison inmates, and enabled Swiss women who'd married foreigners to retain their nationality.

She very quickly got involved in the campaign for women's voting rights. She was one of the women who marched in 1928 during the Swiss National Exhibition, with a huge snail bearing the message: "The march for women's suffrage in Switzerland"—a way of highlighting its slow speed! In 1945, she founded an action committee to support the following premise: Because the constitution states that all Swiss are equal and because women are also Swiss, then those women should have the same rights as the men. Obvious, right? ⟶

Change the law

In 1957, along with the 1,414 members of her association, she requested a voting card from her town. Leaders of the cities and villages refused, and the feminists lodged an appeal, meaning that they requested a new ruling. From appeal to appeal, the case moved all the way up to the federal court, the highest judicial authority in the country. At that point, two of the seven judges agreed that the women were right, which was the start of victory. Finally, the town of Unterbäch in the canton of Valais was the first to allow women to vote; out of the 86 women voters in the town, only 33 dared place a ballot in the box. Many men booed them as they went.

Two years later, Swiss men voted on whether or not to grant Swiss women the right to vote. The majority of the cantons said no, except for Vaud, Geneva, and Neuchatel. Vaud voters also accepted women's suffrage at the cantonal level and the women in this canton became the first in Switzerland to be granted the right to vote.

You've probably heard of Rosa Parks, who became famous after refusing to give up her seat to a white man on an American bus in 1955. Did you know that Ida B. Wells did the same thing, but on a train way back in 1884? She even bit the conductor who tried to throw her from the compartment!

Ida B. Wells was born into a family of slaves who were emancipated, meaning freed, a few months after her birth when President Lincoln abolished slavery in the United States in 1863. She publicly joined the fight for African American rights after what happened on the train. Having become a journalist, she documented the lynching of Black southerners. Lynching is when a person is beaten to death by a group. Many people were lynched by white men simply for being Black, or for speaking to a white woman.

Ida B. Wells didn't like that men acted as if women belonged to the men. She was tired of women being told what to do and who they should spend their time with. So she also got involved in the fight for women's rights. $\longrightarrow$

PUT YOURSELF FORWARD

Convinced that equality would come through voting rights, she protested on behalf of women's suffrage, but this wasn't always so welcome with white women activists. In 1913, she participated in a large march organized in Washington D.C.; she was asked to walk at the back, just like on the trains! Ida refused and stood on the front lines! For her entire life, she fought against racism and sexism by founding organizations, joining in meetings, and writing articles.

In 1930, one year before she died, Ida B. Wells ran for a seat in the Illinois State Senate and became one of the first Black women to stand in an election for public office. She lost, but she paved the way for future generations. In 2020, 70 years after her death, she was awarded a Pulitzer Prize for her courageous journalism about the lynching of Black people.

Qiu Jin was a Chinese poet and revolutionary figure. After being married very young, she quickly left her husband and children, selling her jewelry to pay for her passage to Japan. Once there, she began dressing like a man and carrying a sword. As you may have noticed, most feminists conduct a non-violent fight, but for others, like Emmeline Pankhurst and Qiu Jin, they sometimes had to go a bit further to make their voices heard.

Upon her return to China, she joined up with a group of revolutionary women and founded feminist newspapers, which were all censored by the government. She learned how to make bombs and wrote poems. "Don't tell me that women aren't heroines," she wrote in one.

Qiu Jin fought against arranged marriages and the tradition of foot binding, a practice of wrapping girls' feet to keep them from growing, which was very painful but considered prettier! She fought against a society that kept women inside their homes, and dreamed of setting up a new political regime where women would have the same rights as men.

She became a teacher in one of the country's first schools for girls but continued discreetly to try to overthrow the government. In 1907, she attempted a coup against the Qing Dynasty. She was arrested and beheaded. Chinese women obtained the right to vote in 1953.

WIELD THE SWORD

LUCRETIA MOTT
1793–1880
UNITED STATES

Lucretia Coffin was the daughter of a whaler and a shop owner, and she grew up in a family of American Quakers, which is a religion that believes all are equal before God. At her school, she learned that women were paid less than men. She also learned about the horrors of slavery. Lucretia decided to dedicate herself to these two causes: The rights of women and slaves. Her family's home became a way station on the Underground Railroad—part of the journey taken by slaves who'd escaped from plantations in the American South.

In July 1848, Lucretia Mott—by then she had married James Mott and taken his last name—helped to organize the Seneca Falls Convention for women's rights. Approximately 200 people attended, including 32 men. They drafted "The Declaration of Sentiments." The text demanded that women receive the same rights as men: The right to vote, of course, but also that women could keep their children in the event of a divorce as well as have access to higher education. Slavery was abolished in the United States that same year. White women would have to wait until 1920 for the right to vote, and many African American women until 1965.

Defend the oppressed

KATE SHEPPARD
1847–1934
NEW ZEALAND

Born in England, Kate Sheppard moved to New Zealand in the late 1860s with part of her family. She maintained the view that women must be able to participate in all aspects of life, including politics. She was against the corset that tightened women's waists and constricted their movements. She argued in favor of girls being able to participate in sports and ride bicycles.

At the age of 25, she joined a Christian organization that fought against men's alcoholism and for women's right to vote. She published texts in favor of women's suffrage, organized meetings, and made petitions to be sent to Parliament. The third attempt was successful, especially as the paper was 885 feet long and the suffragists had wrapped it around the building where the representatives were in session! In 1893, New Zealand women were the first on Earth to obtain the right to vote without any conditions attached.

Kate Sheppard continued to fight within her country and for women around the world. She launched *The White Ribbon*—the first newspaper in the country founded, written, and published by women—and increased her international travels. In 1919, New Zealand women earned the right to run for public office.

Have you been to New Zealand? If you go there, you will see a portrait of Kate Sheppard on the country's $10 banknote.

SIGN
A GIANT
PETITION

Whether from New Zealand or China, France or Brazil, or whether they lived in the 18th century or are alive today, these heroines all have a few things in common. Have you noticed some? Often, they had to become independent with respect to their families or husbands, an act which caused a scandal. Often, they created organizations and published texts to increase the visibility of their causes. Often, their fight for women's rights fell within a larger struggle for justice and peace. Olympe de Gouges brought aid to poor people, Huda Sharawi worked to free Egypt from an occupying British power, Lucretia Mott supported the anti-slavery movement... And all too often, these courageous women ended up behind bars.

Sometimes, there were men who supported these pioneers, like:

NICOLAS DE CONDORCET
1743–1794, FRANCE

Celebrated mathematician and philosopher, Nicolas de Condorcet began very early to support women's rights, but also the rights of Jewish people and Blacks. He was what is called a progressive, meaning that he was working toward a more equitable and modern society. He believed that the French Revolution was an opportunity to make his views well-known and published several texts calling for women's suffrage. In his view, a democracy was not truly a democracy until women had the right to vote. And when people told him that women were not intelligent enough, he answered that this was only because they'd been excluded from education and that there were definitely women who were sharper than certain men who, indeed, already had voting rights.

JOHN STUART MILL
1806–1873, GREAT BRITAIN

Extremely inspired by the ideas asserted by his wife, Harriet Taylor Mill, the British economist and philosopher published "The Subjection of Women" in 1869. His text decried the fact that the women in his country paid taxes without having the right to vote. He did not believe there were any innate differences between men and women, only those that came through education and socialization. This meant there was no reason that women should work in service to men by cooking, doing laundry and other tasks. This was a revolutionary notion for the era and is even sometimes still today!

But suffragists were also often faced with the doubts, and the anger, of other women:

GEORGE SAND
1804–1876, FRANCE

Amantine Aurore Lucile Dupin was a feminist. So much so that she separated from her violent, alcoholic husband, at a time when this was not done, and went off to live in Paris. She published novels under the alias George Sand. In French, the masculine first name Georges is usually written with an "s": in this way she kept her name ambiguous. Taking a man's name to write was a relatively common practice at the time because women authors were ignored.

George Sand smoked cigars and dressed as a man. It cost her less money, was more comfortable, and gave her access to places usually off-limits for women, like the general audience section of a theatre, libraries, and courthouses. She had to request permission from the city prefect to wear trousers, something that was granted to French women only during carnival times or for health reasons.

In her books, George Sand defended women's liberation. But she also felt it was too early to claim the right to vote. She believed that women needed to first gain their freedom in order to then become voting citizens.

No matter the time period or the geographic location, the arguments against a woman's right to vote were generally the same:

POSTERS FOR

"A people who are free need women who are free." Switzerland ↑

Cover illustration for the sheet music of Herman Paley and Alfred Bryan's song in support of women's suffrage. USA ↑

USA ↑

A 1915 illustration by Henry Mayer, titled "The Awakening," suggested the geographical force behind the suffrage movement. USA ↑

"Women's vote in Mexico." ↑
"Local votes for women, YES." Switzerland →

POSTERS AGAINST

"Protect her! Political parties, a woman should not be 'preyed upon' by the parties. Vote NO." Switzerland ↑

USA ↑

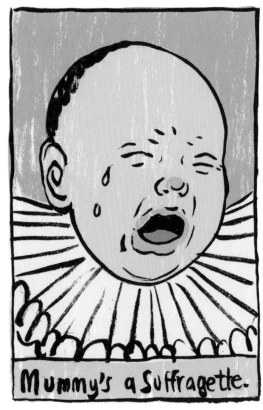

Great Britain ↑

"Popular vote on women's suffrage. What we have. What's at stake." Switzerland ↑

"No to women's suffrage." Switzerland ↑

"No political fights in the home! No women's vote." Switzerland ↑

Great Britain ↑

Notice anything? The individuals who support women's suffrage emphasize the role that women already play in society, the injustice caused by not having the same rights as men, and the partnership between the two sexes.

Oppositely, those who are against the women's right to vote highlight chaos in the home, abandoned children, and the need to protect women from bad influences.

Do your parents vote? If so, does this mean they forget to take care of you?

WHEN DID THEY SUCCEED?

In the 18th century, several countries and regions like Sweden, Corsica, and the province of Lower Canada gave women the right to vote under certain conditions. But it was essentially during the 20th century that most women on the planet became full citizens of their countries. Often, this was accomplished in stages. The first to vote were wealthy and educated, and largely white. Voting rights were only slowly offered to others—first in local elections and then in national ones.

SWEDEN

The "Roddarmadamer" were women who belonged to a guild of professional rowers that ran a water taxi service in and around Stockholm. This type of organization enabled Swedish women in the 18th century to vote.

1718 SWEDEN: A PRECURSOR

In 1718, Sweden became the first country in the world to grant women the right to vote. However, this was subject to certain conditions: Only women who paid taxes and belonged to a guild* could vote, and only in local elections in their city or village.

This right was taken away several years later and then reintroduced, then taken away again and reintroduced with new restrictions... married women, for example, were excluded because they were then considered minors under the responsibility of their husbands. It was finally in 1909 that all Swedish women were given the right to vote in town elections and in 1919 at the national level.

*A guild is an association of individuals who all exercise the same profession, like trade merchants for example.

1893	1901	1906	1913	1915
NEW ZEALAND	AUSTRALIA, EXCEPT FOR ABORIGINAL PEOPLES	FINLAND	NORWAY	ICELAND DENMARK

🔲 WOMEN HAVE JUST EARNED VOTING RIGHTS IN THESE COUNTRIES

A delegation from the Australian Women's Conference in Brisbane, Australia, in 1909.

RUSSIA

CANADA
AUSTRIA
GERMANY
ESTONIA
HUNGARY
KYRGYZSTAN
LATVIA
POLAND

"What gave the October revolution to the factory worker and the peasant woman." Written on the buildings: "Home for women and children," "school for adults," "library," "elementary school," "workers club," and "restaurant." Russia, 1920

1917 RUSSIA: REVOLUTION AT EVERY LEVEL

In 1789, the men who took power in Russia decided, just like their counterparts in France, that women's suffrage was not a priority. They were fighting for more equality between men, but not between women and men. In February 1917, a revolution in which many women participated ended the tsarist regime in Russia. In March of that year, 40,000 women protested in front of parliament, yelling, "A free woman in a free Russia." They succeeded in opening discussions, and then earned the right to vote several weeks later.

Alexandra Kollontai was named People's Commissar for Social Welfare, a ministerial title, and she introduced a series of laws in favor of women: Maternity leave, salary equality, the right to a simpler process of divorce, the right to abortion... This meant that Russia became one of the most advanced countries in terms of equality between women and men.

THE NETHERLANDS   BELARUS
SWEDEN   LUXEMBOURG
UKRAINE

☐ WOMEN ALREADY HAVE VOTING RIGHTS IN THESE COUNTRIES
☐ WOMEN HAVE JUST EARNED VOTING RIGHTS IN THESE COUNTRIES

Marie Juchacz, elected as a representative in 1919, was the first woman to speak in front of the German parliament.

1920

UNITED STATES
ALBANIA
FORMER
CZECHOSLOVAKIA

1921

ARMENIA
AZERBAIJAN

1924

MONGOLIA
KAZAKHSTAN
TAJIKISTAN

Black suffragettes in Georgia, USA, in 1920.

1920 UNITED STATES: FOR FEMINISM AND AGAINST SLAVERY

The fight for women's suffrage in the United States went hand in hand with the fight against slavery: In a democracy, everyone should have the same rights. In 1848, a first convention in the city of Seneca Falls (see Lucretia Mott's story on p. 51) resulted in a declaration in favor of equality between men and women. Many other conventions followed, and several States decided to give voting rights to women.

It wasn't until 1920, after numerous marches, tax protests, and hunger strikes, that women's suffrage was written into the constitution; but even then it was reserved for white women. In 1965, American men and women, no matter the color of their skin, were finally given the right to vote.

1927 — TURKMENISTAN URUGUAY

1928 — GREAT BRITAIN

1929 — ECUADOR ROMANIA

☐ WOMEN ALREADY HAVE VOTING RIGHTS IN THESE COUNTRIES
☐ WOMEN HAVE JUST EARNED VOTING RIGHTS IN THESE COUNTRIES

THE CAT AND MOUSE ACT
PASSED BY THE LIBERAL GOVERNMENT

THE LIBERAL CAT
ELECTORS VOTE AGAINST HIM!
KEEP THE LIBERAL OUT!

In Great Britain, imprisoned suffragettes used hunger strikes as a form of protest. A law was voted in 1913 enabling them to be freed as soon as their health was threatened and then re-imprisoned once they were better—a bit like a cat playing with a mouse, setting it free and then catching it again. This poster denounced the liberal government that had enacted the law.

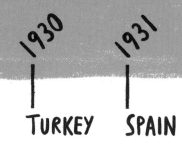

Women walking with their faces uncovered, a sign of modernity in Turkey in 1932.

1930 TURKEY: LIBERATED WOMEN IN A SECULAR SOCIETY

In 1923, the Ottoman Empire gave way, after centuries of power, to the new Republic of Turkey. President Mustafa Kemal, later renamed Atatürk, dreamt of modernizing the country according to a Western model. The image of the liberated woman became his banner, meaning it was a kind of advertisement for his secular* policies. Young women were granted the right to study. The Civil Code, which was inspired by Swiss law, ended polygamy—the possibility for a man to have several wives—and granted women the rights to divorce and equal inheritance. In 1930, they obtained the right to vote and to stand in municipal elections. In 1934, that right was extended to national elections.

*A secular country is one in which religion is kept separate from political power.

1932

BRAZIL
MALDIVES
THAILAND

1934

CUBA

1937

PHILIPPINES

☐ WOMEN ALREADY HAVE VOTING RIGHTS IN THESE COUNTRIES
☐ WOMEN HAVE JUST EARNED VOTING RIGHTS IN THESE COUNTRIES

A Brazilian woman exercising her recently earned right to vote in 1932.

Louise Weiss and her protest companions, to the left behind the microphone and in front of the Eiffel Tower, during the 1937 International Exposition of Art and Technology in Modern Life in Paris.

1944 FRANCE: IMPACT OF WAR

In 1848, France instituted a "universal" right to vote—until this point voting was reserved for those who paid taxes—but in truth, women were excluded. In 1919, representatives authorized French women to vote but the senators refused. And in France a law can only be instituted when both assemblies have ratified it. The same situation occurred in 1925, 1932, and 1935! It wasn't until 1944, in a country destroyed by war, that women finally earned the right to vote. The senators finally gave in following the massive involvement of French women in the workplace and in the Resistance.

ITALY
CAMEROON

☐ WOMEN ALREADY HAVE VOTING RIGHTS IN THESE COUNTRIES
☐ WOMEN HAVE JUST EARNED VOTING RIGHTS IN THESE COUNTRIES

Japanese women dropping off their ballots for a school election during the era of the modernist Emperor Taisho (1912–1926). It wasn't until 1947 that all Japanese women unequivocally obtained the right to vote.

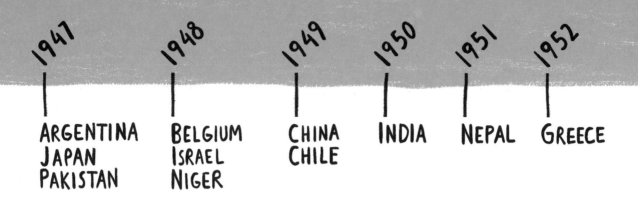

1947 — ARGENTINA JAPAN PAKISTAN

1948 — BELGIUM ISRAEL NIGER

1949 — CHINA CHILE

1950 — INDIA

1951 — NEPAL

1952 — GREECE

1947 ARGENTINA: AN INFLUENTIAL WOMAN

In Argentina, the wife of the country's new president Juan Perón, worked openly in favor of women's right to vote, even if feminists had been preparing the ground for her for decades. Eva Perón, nicknamed Evita, declared that women should vote and also that they should vote for women. The Parliament refused, but she insisted and kept insisting. In 1947, women's suffrage was finally adopted. It was enacted during the general elections of 1951 and 90% of the country's women showed up at the ballot box.

1953   1954   1955   1956   1957   1958

MEXICO   COLOMBIA   PERU   TOGO   LEBANON   BURKINA FASO
SYRIA   BELIZE   EGYPT   GUINEA
                    SOMALIA   CHAD

☐ WOMEN ALREADY HAVE VOTING RIGHTS IN THESE COUNTRIES
☐ WOMEN HAVE JUST EARNED VOTING RIGHTS IN THESE COUNTRIES

In Peru, the presidential elections of 1956 was the first time women widely participated in the country's political life.

1961
PARAGUAY
RWANDA

1962
ALGERIA
MONACO

1963
AFGHANISTAN
IRAN

1967
CONGO

A voting office in French-speaking Switzerland in 1970: At this point, women were still only allowed to vote for local issues and in certain cantons.

1971 SWITZERLAND: A DECISION OF THE PEOPLE

People often make fun of Switzerland because women obtained the right to vote so late. And it's true: It took until 1991 for every single Swiss woman to become a voting citizen! A small consolation prize is that Switzerland was the only country in the world to achieve women's suffrage via popular vote.

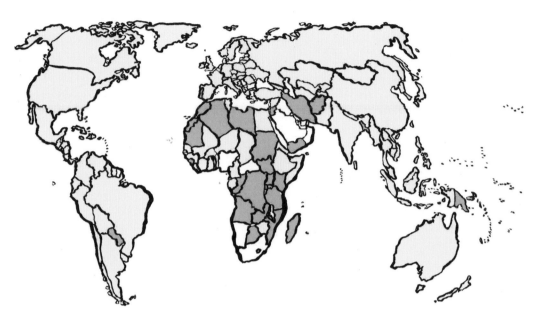

1971 SWITZERLAND   **1976** PORTUGAL

☐ WOMEN ALREADY HAVE VOTING RIGHTS IN THESE COUNTRIES

▣ WOMEN HAVE JUST EARNED VOTING RIGHTS IN THESE COUNTRIES

Protest by the Women's Liberation Movement in Lisbon's Parque Eduardo VII in 1974.

Women braving the rain in Lagos in 1979 to give their votes.

1979 NIGERIA: IN THE NAME OF TRADITION

As is often the case, mobilization began in a city—in Nigeria's capital Lagos. What was the women's main argument here? Tradition, because before the country had been colonized by the British, women had enjoyed a greater degree of power. In 1950, they obtained the right to vote if they were paying taxes, but most women were not taxpayers. In 1953, they organized a Women's Parliament to be held in parallel to a conference that brought together British colonials and Nigerian politicians in London to revise the constitution. But this wasn't enough. Finally, in 1979, a democracy was established, and Nigerian women became full citizens of their country.

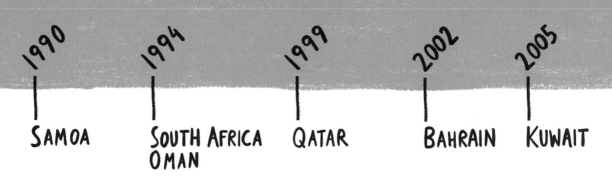

☐ WOMEN ALREADY HAVE VOTING RIGHTS IN THESE COUNTRIES
☐ WOMEN HAVE JUST EARNED VOTING RIGHTS IN THESE COUNTRIES

South African poster from 1994 encouraging women to keep fighting for more rights, now that women's suffrage had been achieved.

81

Saudi Arabia

A Saudi Arabian woman voter during the local elections held at the end of 2015.

2011 SAUDI ARABIA : AT THE WHIM OF THE KING

In 2011, King Abdullah of Saudi Arabia granted women the right to vote and to stand in local elections. But there is no parliament and women have very few rights. They must, for example, be completely veiled in public and many professions are off limits to them.

A FEW HOLDOUTS

Nowadays, women vote almost everywhere in the world, with two notable exceptions. The first is Brunei, a small Southeast Asian state with an absolute monarchy. The sultan retains all powers, and no one has the right to vote, not even the men. The other location is the Vatican, in Rome, a micro-state that functions as the headquarters of the Roman Catholic Church. Here, the cardinals vote to elect the pope, and the bishops make decisions regarding church directives. Since women are not allowed to become priests, bishops, or cardinals, they are excluded from all decision-making. But the revolution is making small inroads even here: In early 2021, the nun Nathalie Becquart was nominated under-secretary to the Assembly of Bishops and can now participate in voting.

HAS THERE EVER BEEN A WOMAN PRESIDENT?

Of course, there have been women presidents, although this is a "rare species" compared to the much more commonly spotted presidential man. Women presidents are often thought of in a slightly different way, too. You'll see.

WOMEN HEADS OF STATE

The first woman in the world to become a president was Isabel Martinez de Perón. This was in 1974, in Argentina. She was vice president when her husband, the president, passed away; she became his successor. But the first woman president elected via universal suffrage* was Vigdís Finnbogadóttir in 1980.

It's no accident that the first woman president was Icelandic as this beautiful northern island has a long history of a better equality between men and women. Vigdís Finnbogadóttir remembers her first day as president: "During my inauguration ceremony, I was alone in the middle of an assembly of men in suits, a woman surrounded by penguins! It was astonishing!"

*Universal suffrage is when an entire population has the right to vote.

After her came Corazon Aquino in the Philippines in 1986, Ellen Johnson Sirleaf in Liberia in 2006, and Sahle-Work Zewde in Ethiopia in 2018. There have been about 20 women presidents in all, and many more as interim heads of state—which happens when a president steps down a bit too quickly and a replacement hasn't yet been selected. How interesting! Women are more readily given power on a provisory basis or to handle a crisis. This is also true in the business world.

MAP SHOWING THE COUNTRIES THAT SINCE THEIR INDEPENDENCE HAVE HAD AT LEAST (EXCLUDING QUEENS)...

 a woman as head of government

 a woman as head of state

 a woman holding both offices as head of government and head of state

 a woman as head of state and a woman as head of government

WOMEN HEADS OF GOVERNMENT

In many countries, the head of government has more power than the president.

The first women prime ministers were elected starting in 1960 in Sri Lanka, in India, and then in Israel. But the first woman who often comes to mind is Margaret Thatcher, perhaps because she was the prime minister of the United Kingdom from 1979 to 1990. Eleven years is a long time. Or maybe because she was nicknamed, "The Iron Lady?" Margaret Thatcher was a hardliner in business affairs, whether this involved negotiating with strikers or with the European Union.

How about Angela Merkel? Do you know her? She was also in power for many years as German Chancellor from 2005 to the end of 2021. She was trained as a physicist and perhaps that helped her adapt to different situations. She knew how to make compromises, and take "small steps." This meant handling one problem after another. She will be remembered for having welcomed a million migrants in 2015, most of them Syrian refugees, while many other countries were closing their borders. Germans call her "Mutti," which means "mommy" in German. A little cliché, don't you think?

A prime minister who really knocked people's socks off is Jacinda Ardern. She's been the head of the New Zealand government since 2017, a position she earned at the fairly young age of 37. She is generally lauded for her calm approach in difficult situations; she continued answering interview questions, for example, during an earthquake! The video went viral on social media platforms. In 2020, her handling of the Covid-19 situation ensured her country did better than many others during the pandemic.

Jacinda Ardern became a mother during her first term; this scandalized many people who felt she couldn't manage both a country and a child. She proved the opposite to be true and even attended a United Nations assembly with her infant in her arms. When journalists asked her whether it was fair to question a woman about her maternity plans during a hiring process, she replied: "It is totally unacceptable in 2017 to say that women should have to answer that question in the workplace, it is unacceptable, it is unacceptable." No one, in fact, asked former French president Nicolas Sarkozy the same question when his daughter was born.

In the United States in early 2021, Kamala Harris became the first woman vice president as well as the first mixed-race woman in this role. She even became the first woman to hold presidential powers in the USA (for 1 hour and 25 minutes on November 19, 2021) when she stood in for President Joe Biden while he underwent a medical procedure.

And let's also note that in 2020, Petra De Sutter became the Belgian deputy prime minister and Sarah McBride became an American senator. Why the fuss? Both are transgender women.

METTE FREDERIKSEN
PM DENMARK

KATRÍN JAKOBSDÓTTIR
PM ICELAND

MAGDALENA
ANDERSSON
PM SWEDEN

SANNA MARIN
PM FINLAND

INGRIDA ŠIMONYTĖ
PM LITHUANIA

URSULA VON DER LEYEN
PRESIDENT OF THE
EUROPEAN COMMISSION

ROBERTA METSOLA
PRESIDENT OF THE
EUROPEAN PARLIAMENT

MIA MOTTLEY
PM BARBADOS

ANA BRNABIĆ
PM SERBIA

VJOSA OSMANI
PR KOSOVO

PAULA-MAE WEEKES
PR TRINIDAD AND TOBAGO

VICTOIRE TOMEGAH DOGBÉ
PM TOGO

ROSE CHRISTIANE
OSSOUKA RAPONDA
PR GABON

SAARA
KUUGONGELWA-AMADHILA
PM NAMIBIA

KATERINA
SAKELLAROPOULOU
PR GREECE

KAJA KALLAS
PM ESTONIA

NAJLA BOUDEN
PM TUNISIA

THE 27 WOMEN HEADS OF GOVERNMENT AROUND THE WORLD (JANUARY 2022)

PR- PRESIDENT
PM - PRIME MINISTER

ZUZANA ČAPUTOVÁ
PR SLOVAKIA

SALOME ZOURABICHVILI
PR GEORGIA

TSAI ING-WEN
PR TAIWAN

SHEIKH HASINA
PM BANGLADESH

MAIA SANDU
PR MOLDOVA

BIDHYA DEVI BHANDARI
PR NEPAL

SAHLE-WORK ZEWDE
PR ETHIOPIA

HALIMAH YACOB
PR SINGAPORE

SAMIA SULUHU HASSAN
PR TANZANIA

JACINDA ARDERN
PM NEW ZEALAND

MINISTERS

Most of the world's ministers, meaning the members of the government, are men. But the number of women is increasing—21.3% in 2020.

In 2018, nine countries achieved parity, which means they included the same number of men as women in the government. Among the nine are Costa Rica, Ethiopia, Rwanda, and the Seychelles. This represents 6% of the governments in the world.

In 2020, there were 14!

Some ministries remain relatively inaccessible to women. The departments of finance or defense are male bastions* while family and social affairs, the environment, or education are more often given to women politicians. In the United States, Bill Clinton, George W. Bush, and Barack Obama all nominated women to important cabinet positions, but two departments have always been run by men: defense and veterans affairs.

In 2020, nine countries still had never had a single woman minister: Saudi Arabia, Brunei, Kiribati, Papua New Guinea, Saint-Vincent and the Grenadines, Thailand, Tuvalu, Vanuatu, and Vietnam. Would you know where to find them on a map?

*A bastion is a fortress, meaning a place that is more difficult to conquer than others.

"THE JUPPETTES"

In 1995 in France, Prime Minister Alain Juppé very proudly announced that nearly a third of his government was composed of women. Twelve women were nominated, but to secretary of state positions—which are lower than ministerial positions—or to lesser valued ministries like tourism or health. They were ironically called "the juppettes" (a pun meaning "the little skirts" made from the PM's last name) and were let go six months after they took their positions.

FIRST COUNTRY
IN THE WORLD
WITH A WOMAN
**PRIME
MINISTER:**

(SRI LANKA)

**SIRIMAVO
BANDARANAIKE,
1960**

FIRST COUNTRY
IN THE WORLD
WITH A WOMAN
PRESIDENT:

(ICELAND)

**VIGDÍS
FINNBOGADÓTTIR,
1980**

FIRST COUNTRY
IN THE WORLD
WITH A MAJORITY
**WOMEN
PARLIAMENT:**

(RWANDA)

2008

PROPORTION OF WOMEN REPRESENTATIVES

1945 — 3%
1965 — 8%
1985 — 12%
2005 — 16%
2021 — 25.5%

WOMEN REPRESENTATIVES

In April 2021, 25.5% of the world's elected representatives were women, meaning a quarter! Representatives are the people who create a country's laws. Rwanda (61.3% women), Cuba (53.4%) and the United Arab Emirates (50%) have the best scores in this category. If we look by region, the Nordic countries are at the top of the list with a rate of 44.5%. In the Middle East and in northern Africa, it drops to 17.7%, and in the Pacific Islands (excluding Australia and New Zealand) it drops to 6.4%.

Hoping to improve women's participation in political life, some countries have introduced quotas, which means that a proportion of the available seats must go to women. But this method can cause criticism and sometimes doesn't even work because the quota is not respected or because the women elected in this way are not taken seriously.

WHO WILL TAKE CARE OF THE CHILDREN?

Unfortunately, once elected, women are often treated differently. The media will more readily call them by their first name while men are often referred to by their last name. When they appear in public, their clothing is often commented on, something which male politicians rarely experience. In 2012, newly elected French Housing Minister Cécile Duflot was whistled at when she wore a dress to the National Assembly gallery. And many people made jokes about all the different colored suits Angela Merkel wore.

Women are often judged by their appearance and must fight to be heard and taken seriously. They are also punished for being mothers—and considered to be bad mothers when they decide to put their careers first or try to combine their political and family lives. Pregnant ministers, for example, have been singled out for abuse from France to New Zealand and even in Ireland.

In 2006, when Ségolène Royal announced her candidacy for the French presidential election, and her husband was the first secretary of the Socialist Party at the time, another politician asked, "Who will take care of the children?" Do I even need to mention again that no one ever asks male candidates this question?

Indeed, an interesting study from 2008 shows that "family" was cited as the first barrier for women who wanted to begin or make a career in politics.

THE FIVE MAIN FACTORS STOPPING WOMEN AND MEN FROM ENGAGING IN POLITICS

FACTORS FOR WOMEN	FACTORS FOR MEN
Family responsibilities	Lack of electoral support
Dominant cultural perception of the role of women in society	Lack of money
Lack of family support	Lack of political party support
Lack of confidence	Lack of experience in "representative functions": public speaking, relationships with electors
Lack of money	Lack of confidence

Source: IPU, Equality in Politics. A Survey of Women and Men in Parliaments, 2008.

GOVERN LIKE A MAN?

It's true that many men in the past believed that women were not fit to vote, and even more men believed a woman would be incapable of governing.

This means that many women politicians have admitted they needed to adopt "masculine" behaviors in a bid for greater respect. Some women even took classes to lower their voices and speak in a more measured way, like Margaret Thatcher in the United Kingdom and Ségolène Royal in France.

But some women politicians have been praised for not conducting business as usual—a consequence of their upbringing. At the beginning of the Covid-19 pandemic, for example, studies showed that countries governed by women had better results. One British study calculated that these women-led countries recorded half as many deaths. Why? Essentially because they went into lockdown faster. What would you choose—health or the economy?

Sources: IPU, iknowpolitics, ONU, RTS.

WHAT'S NEXT?

Over the past 50 years, the fight for women's equality has gained great momentum: The right to vote, to study, to travel... But there are still some areas that need more work. Here are a few examples.

SALARIES

In the United States and France, the differences between men's and women's salaries can be as great as 20%. This means that for every man who earns $10, every woman receives only $8, even though she works in the same job. And this difference climbs to 33% when the figures include the entire world. Studies have also shown that very large salaries are mostly paid to men and very low salaries to women. Not very fair, right? Just imagine if parents gave a different allowance to their boys versus their girls of the same age...

HOUSEHOLD TASKS

Here, too, the figures are very clear. On average, in both the United States and the European Union, women are responsible for two-thirds of household chores compared to one-third for men. Women spend at least an hour a day on these tasks, which is not the case for most of their companions, and it gets worse in certain countries. Who does what in your house? The younger generations are more accustomed to sharing household tasks than older ones. You might have noticed that your father knows how to cook or do the laundry but there's a chance your grandfather does not! But often, even within more egalitarian couples, the arrival of a child upsets the balance.

CHILDREN

Not so long ago, it was believed that only women could take care of children, certainly because they gave birth to them and often breastfed them. Today, it seems clear that fathers know how to care for children too, but many continue to spend less time with their children than the mothers. Who sorts out the clothing that's gotten too small and buys new ones? Who thinks of birthday gifts for the friends of their children? All these tasks and responsibilities combined are what is called the "mental load."

It is a problem when society assigns this role to mothers. For example, when a child is ill and the school gets in touch with the mother and not the father, this makes people think it's alright to bother a woman at work, but not a man.

LANGUAGE

You're lucky because English is a fairly inclusive language! Most of the names of the professions don't have a feminine or masculine form, and the pronoun "they" is already widely used to avoid distinguishing between "she" and "he." Other neutral forms were also invented over recent decades, like "Mx." instead of "Mr." or "Mrs."

This isn't true for other languages. In French, for example, most of the nouns used for the different professions change depending on whether the word is used with respect to a man or a woman, and in a mixed setting the masculine form is used for a group of men AND women. This is because grammarians decided to favor masculine forms in the 17th century, because they believed that "the male is superior to the female."

Studies have shown that this is a problem. When we hear the word "superheroes," the image that comes to mind is a group of men. This is why in the United States, we try to use words like "firefighter" instead of "fireman" or "police officer" instead of "policeman." Many people would like to amend the US Constitution, which still uses "he" when talking about the president!

Feminists support inclusive language so that everyone feels included and can find their role in society. The idea is that if language shapes how we see the world, we need to make language more equal to promote a fairer society.

This can sometimes create heated debates. There are many who argue against adopting these changes on the grounds that they are ugly, restrictive, and useless. Others contend that equality between human beings is worth this small effort.

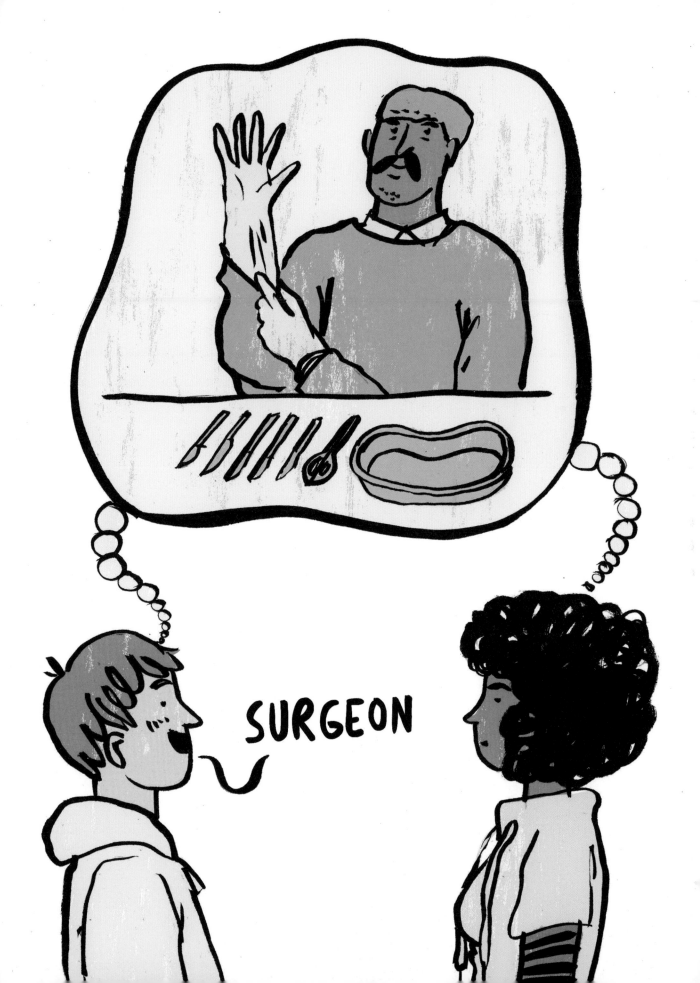

MUSEUM

Positions of Power

As you read in the last chapter, women remain in the minority as heads of state. The same thing is true in business. In early 2021 in France, for example, there was only one woman CEO among the 40 largest companies. This is also true for religious organizations; except for a few women pastors, Anglican bishops, rabbis, and imams, the leadership positions within the Catholic, Jewish, Muslim and even Buddhist faiths are overwhelmingly filled by men.

Another example: Most of the artists exhibited in museums and who earn prizes are men, and yet the majority of art students are women. This is even more unfortunate because these positions of power are what make it possible for a situation to change.

MENSTRUATION

Menstruation remains a taboo everywhere in the world and this has serious consequences. In Myanmar, for example, teen girls are often forbidden from going out of the house on the days they have their periods. They are considered unclean and impure, and this affects their self-esteem. They miss a week of school each month, which affects their academic achievements. They are unable to frequently change their sanitary pads because they don't have enough money or the help they need. This effects their health. A heated debate in many countries these days is whether it's a good idea to install machines to distribute sanitary pads in schools. Some cultures remain superstitious about menstruation, believing that a woman on her period shouldn't be allowed to cook or care for plants.

THE RIGHT TO CONTROL OVER ONE'S OWN BODY

Several of the world's countries have traditions that weigh heavily on women's bodies. In many countries in central and northern Africa, most girls undergo "female genital mutilation," which is a painful and harmful operation on girls' vaginas. In Malaysia and Bangladesh, many young girls are married against their will, often to much older men. In Saudi Arabia and Iran, they are unable to leave the house without covering themselves with a veil, sometimes completely. In France, those who choose to wear a veil cannot become civil servants or teachers. In Qatar, a woman who is raped may be condemned for having an extramarital sexual relationship. In many countries around the world, if a woman becomes pregnant and does not want to have a baby, she has no choice, or anyone to turn to for help. And that is true even if she was raped, or if there are problems with the pregnancy and the baby has no hope of surviving.

And in almost every country, women are told what they can or cannot wear. Some women have to disguise their nipples under their swimsuits by wearing stickers on their breasts. In many places, teenage girls who show their shoulders, legs or bellies are told they shouldn't dress like that. In short, too many men believe they have the right to police the bodies of women or use them as they wish, instead of changing their own behavior.

ESTABLISHED ROLES

Have you noticed that some toys are for boys and others for girls, some books for boys and others for girls, some magazines for boys and others for girls, and even certain clothing is for boys and others for girls? This is what's called gendered marketing and its goal is to increase sales. For example, if parents and children are convinced that pink bicycles are better for girls, then they need to buy a blue, green, or black one for a little brother, instead of handing down a big sister's bicycle.

During the Covid-19 pandemic there were even green hand sanitizing gels for boys named "Desinfector" and pink ones for girls named "Little Princesses." This has another impact in the sense that boys are associated with active superheroes and girls with passive little dolls. By repeating and reinforcing these stereotypes, we validate the idea that boys must be strong, brave, and active, while girls are better suited to take care of others and households. In the long run, this makes us think that women can't run businesses and men can't do a good job caring for children.

DEAR READERS

I learned so much while writing this book, and I hope you've learned while reading it.

I realized exactly how far we've come in 150 years, but also how much further there is still to go. Olympe, Emmeline, Huda, we owe you so much! And your fight continues to strongly echo alongside ours in the 21st century. You fought for a more inclusive society for women, and also for poor people and slaves, in the same way that today's feminists target sexism, racism, homophobia, and transphobia. You were concerned with building fairer states just as feminists today fight for environmentally friendly models of living.

You were called all sorts of names: Harpies, loonies, hysterics, and witches. Just like the women today who step out of established frameworks. And yet your cause–women's voting rights–seems so normal to us that no one questions it— not openly, anyway. I have an immense respect for the anger of protestors, and for the courage of those who change the world. In 50 or 100 years, how will people look back at our struggles?

Dear readers, boys and girls, I hope you will grow up in a world in which all children have the same rights from the very beginning and can choose for themselves the roles they want to have in their homes and in society.

Dear Dune and Salomé, I hope you will grow old in a world in which being born a girl has no negative impact on your career, your daily life, or your relationships. I hope it is a world in which the word "feminism" is no longer frightening.

CAROLINE

EXTRAS

Tests and games for fun and to make you
think, plus some tips to keep learning.

QUIZ

What was the first country to give women the right to vote?

- Switzerland
- Sweden
- Australia

To what do New Zealand women owe their right to vote?

- A 885-foot-long petition
- A bomb
- Patience

What were British protestors called when protesting for the right to vote?

- Suffragettes
- Sufferers
- Statuettes

Are there still countries where women cannot vote?

- Yes
- No

Who was Margaret Thatcher ?

- The President of the United States
- The Queen of England
- The Prime Minister of the United Kingdom

Vigdís Finnbogadóttir is known as:

- Boxing champion
- The first woman president elected via universal suffrage
- Minister of the Vatican

When did all Swiss women finally earn the right to vote?

- 1912
- 1971
- 1991

Women are a majority in parliaments around the world:

- True
- False

Which of the following countries have had a woman president:

- Argentina
- France
- Liberia
- The United States
- Switzerland

Will there be more women presidents than men presidents one day?

- Of course
- Impossible
- I hope so

DIFFERENCES

SLOGANS

Many different slogans have been devised in support of the women's right to vote or, oppositely, to ridicule the idea.

Which ones do you think really existed?

You can also make some up!

DON'T TEAR FAMILIES APART

WOMEN MUST VOTE TO PREVENT WAR

USUALLY WE CLEAN UP, BUT TODAY WE'RE SHAKING THINGS UP
STAY IN YOUR KITCHENS
DEEDS, NOT WORDS

ANSWERS

Quiz: Sweden – Petition – Suffragettes – Yes – The Prime Minister of the United Kingdom – The first woman president elected via universal suffrage – 1991 – False – Argentina, Liberia, Switzerland.

Seven differences: The person reading the newspaper, the newspaper photos, the person doing housework, the television, the girl's t-shirt, the truck, the doll.

Slogans: These truly existed: "Don't break up families"; "Women must vote to prevent war"; "Deeds, not words" (this was the suffragettes' slogan). "Usually we clean up, but today we're shaking things up!" was also used, but later on. You can still see this at feminist protests.

VOCABULARY

Ballot: The little slip of paper placed in a ballot box to vote, for people or for issues.

Ballot box: Receptable used to collect ballots.

Candidates: The individuals who run in elections.

Citizen: Originally used to designate who had a right to vote, used today to describe the inhabitant of a country.

Parliament: Assembly of elected representatives in charge of representing the people.

Representatives: Elected individuals who vote on laws.

Suffrage: The right to vote.

Term of office: A function granted by electors for a specified length of time. For example, a person is elected for one term to be mayor of a town or the president of a country.

Universal suffrage: When every citizen has the right to vote.

Voting booth: Small cabin or stalls where people go to cast their vote in secret.

ACKNOWLEDGMENTS—CAROLINE

I thank my mother for teaching me to be a feminist, often unknowingly; my daughters for taking up the torch so joyfully; Hadi Barkat for his enthusiasm and trust; Ines Djender, Alizée Dabert, Corinne Grandjean, Beatrice Kammener, Aude Pidoux and Richard Harvell for their professional editing; Michelle Bailat-Jones for her translation; Dune Stevan and Paloma Decours-Jaquet for their careful reading; Valérie Vuille from the Association DécadréE for her involved reading; and, finally, Elīna Brasliņa who made these women and eras so vibrant.

ACKNOWLEDGMENTS—ELĪNA

Like Caroline, I give huge thanks to my mother for her wisdom, love, and support; to Hadi who trusted me (for the second time); to my daughter who very much wanted to help me with my drawings; to all the women in my life who are proud to be "feminists," even when it's used as an insult (Santa, Mētra, Agra, Alise, Vivianna, Jana, and so many more); and to Caroline for the power of her writing—this book was a joy to illustrate.

CAROLINE STEVAN

has been voting since her 18th birthday, in Switzerland and in France. She studied political science and journalism and then worked for the Swiss daily newspaper, *Le Temps*, in the international and culture sections. She began working for RTS radio in 2019 and is co-animator of the podcast "Le Point J" and co-programer of the photography festival Alt+1000. She dreams of the day when the word feminism might lose its sting. *Citizen She!* is her third book for Helvetiq, following *Blablacar, la France et moi*, and *Be my quarantine* with Marko Stevic.

ELĪNA BRASLIŅA

is an illustrator from Riga, in Latvia. She has illustrated over 20 books: mainly children's stories and novels by Latvian writers. She also illustrated Lawrence Schimel's board books *Bedtime, Not Playtime!* and *Early One Morning*; Kate Wakeling's poetry collections *Moon Juice* and *Cloud Soup*; and Patricia Forde's picture book *Imagine!* She also creates animated films and feminist art in her free time. *Citizen She!* is the second book she has illustrated for Helvetiq. The first was *Ting!*

EDUCATOR'S GUIDE
HOW DO YOU FIT INTO THE GLOBAL STORY OF WOMEN'S VOTING RIGHTS? REFLECT, CONNECT, AND ACT TO FIND OUT!

REFLECT

- This book begins with a scene in a classroom. Did you find the scene surprising or familiar? Write a paragraph that explains your reaction.
- The author writes that "A ballot is a tiny piece of paper with incredible power!" Create a list of five things a person can do with the power of the ballot.

CONNECT

- Choose your favorite biography from the chapter "How Did They Fight for It?" Then, take a closer look at the "Protestors' Toolkit" on pages 36 and 37. Create a chart with two columns to show which tactics from the toolkit that woman used to fight for the right to vote and why you think those tactics were successful.
- Women often campaigned for suffrage along with other human rights and issues. Why do you think this is the case? Explore the biographies and timelines to find three to five examples of this connection.

ACT

- Even if you aren't old enough to vote, you have a powerful voice. Do you notice an issue in your school or community that needs a new solution? Write to your school principal, school board, local representatives, or local newspaper to share your ideas.
- Gather family and friends to attend a rally or march in support of the rights and well-being of women. Then, consider organizing your own event about some of the challenges still faced by women around the world. Reread "What Else?" on pages 104 to 118 to get inspired!